HE LEAVES HIS FACE IN THE FUNERAL CAR

Caitlin Press Inc.
8100 Alderwood Road,
Halfmoon Bay, BC V0N 1Y1
www.caitlin-press.com

Text and cover design by Vici Johnstone
Cover art by Arleigh Wood
Printed in Canada

Caitlin Press Inc. acknowledges financial support from the Government of
Canada and the Canada Council for the Arts, and from the Province of British
Columbia through the British Columbia Arts Council and the Book Publisher's
Tax Credit.

Library and Archives Canada Cataloguing in Publication

Paré, Arleen, author

He leaves his face in the funeral car / Arleen Paré.

Poems.

ISBN 978-1-927575-92-5 (paperback)

I. Title.

PS8631.A7425H45 2015   C811'.6   C2015-904042-6

He Leaves His Face in the Funeral Car

Arleen Paré

Caitlin Press

For my mother and father, Irene and Tom McCart, whom I miss.

CONTENTS

I

II

I

IF THIS TURNS INTO STORY IT'S GONE TOO FAR

They were butchering a sprawled deer
big as a Beauty Queen right there
on the counter where we lined up to order food.

The full length
                    of the deer's curvaceous thigh
viscera-bright in the corner
of my left eye. Earlier

I'd signed the email
to protest the slaughter of Calderon dolphins,
their slit red throats gleaming dark as knives churning
in the sky-blue Danish bay.

                    Later, at Helen's grocery store,
white curtains lace the windows,
and frilly kale emerald-greens all the bins.

AFTER SUDDEN RAIN

droplets light the mid-pane of my bedroom window
only that pane   the rain that fast   precise

beyond the window   hydro wires bisect the maple tree
whose tips thin out to red

beyond the maple a quarter rainbow clichés the sky
the clichéd sky rummages between violet and green

sun surprises the eye   dries the sidewalk
saturates the buds on the viburnum

cars flash chrome   doors yellow
a man leaves his house in orange trousers

white trim partitions one house from another
a small dog at the end of a leash   a child in a pink hat

the street washes itself in detail
almost too much clarity   optimism

to say the street below approximates perfection
is to celebrate the imperfect   to say the line of rooftops

reaches towards infinity
                              pins the eye to the horizon

tell me   is the desire for originality
original sin   wanting all things new again?

but who can help it   who refuses paradise
when sunlight hallelujahs after sudden rain?

PEAR TREE IN WINTER

What you hope for hangs by a hook
as the iron porch bell hangs
from its wooden jut,
its neck noosed round with rope
waiting for the clang. Time
is how you stand outside yourself
waiting to get in.
Marsh marigold, red-stemmed in cold, waits
for its summer petals, its head golden as if it were
prized, its leaves paired,
companioned.
                    While pears like small lanterns
still hang inside the tree's bare branches,
exactly as they do each year
as if they'd never left,
as if you'd never
gone away.
                    Twelve pears, the iron bell
suspended; time seeping through your fingers.
Soapberries dot the leafless twigs.
The stone Buddha sits on the too-green moss,
moss hugs the rock.
Rust gathers on the axe head. Rust
lines the pit of the barrow which leans on the rail.
The bell waits. Smoke plumes the sky,
and light lowers itself,
the way a woman
lowers herself
into a lake.

HOWEVER, I MISS MY MOTHER

no one knew my mother wore false teeth
until the day my sister
                    saw my mother's empty mouth
after the surgery for cancer   my mother in the ICU
and still asleep

my sister didn't tell me   not for years
she claimed not even my father knew

he left his own teeth on the dresser overnight

when we played Wolf at bedtime
he loosened his uppers to splay a feral promise
my mother warning him
                        . stop   they'll never sleep
he mussed his hair to hackles
us girls on the sofa   screaming

when I was six my mother whispered
your father is a Catholic
we were in the garden at the time
I was not to tell another soul
strange weight   I could not put it down

the surgeon cut my mother open
and closed her up again   the cancer
having gone too far beyond her tarry lungs
having wrapped itself in secret
around her kind clandestine heart

AUBADE FOR THE PATIENT IN BED NUMBER FOUR

my aunt's not crazy but she's crazy
for the wall in the hall outside her room
                    talks about it all the time
that pink   paler than the palest conch shell
or swimming scallop

                                if she cranes her neck
she can glimpse the wall through her cornered sightline
bed four to door

she can't remember how she ended up in room 110
or when or what went wrong

                        it's been a month
the days gather odours she can no longer name

she spent last night in a ship's hold
lying on a door she said   the night before
she taped a sign in a shop window   *open for business*
she knows she's reached the bottom

the colour on the wall outside her room is not paint
or a stain
                it's a wash of light   a luminescence
cast by the overhead fluorescent tubes

she's had a stroke   her mind moves now
in unchartable directions

today she gave me her watch

she still has stories
but the tubes get in the way

on board the ship
men tramped beside her ear
she yanked the hem of the bosun's trousers
asked where and how she got there
the Indian Ocean he said
      he could not tell her how

shrouded now   anything could be a trick   trompe l'oeil
contingent on sightlines   perspectives   angles of uncertain faith

she's old   liminal   she lives in a space between worlds
asks for little   eats next to nothing
dreams of cargo ships and talks about the wall
outside her room   faint echo
a sailor's warning

THESE ARE THE TRIALS OF WATER

That it weeps:
from sunless walls, silvering the grief of stone.
Weeps from newborn eyes, from sliced and salted
eggplant, bitter amber beads.
For anything that's lost.

That it seeps: unwanted,
oozes black from the faulted floors of basements,
cracks and caves and broken seams. Seeps from welts
and sores; seeps
and puddles fingers in the grave.

That it stains: beds and books,
pages waved with traceries of damp; tables, party rings
permanent on the Duncan Phyfe; stains a skirt of froth
around a flooded room.

That it stinks: huddles in brackish holes,
stagnates in hollows. Takes on the stench,
garbage in a gutter, the reek of pain, boils, bile.
Bruises
under the weight of any country's sky.

Water is biblical—in every way
it must be tested.
Let frogs and the eggs of frogs in jellied sacs.
Let faeces, DDT, muck, all manner of larvae.
Let mayflies.
Crayfish, mallards, rainbow trout,
viridescent slime. Water, tainted,
is poisoned, poisons, cannot say no.

Lays itself down in lowlands, in alluvial plains,
in sewers, at the bottom of old wells,
quiet and still. Accepts its state;
does not complain or seek sympathy.
Crashes from plastic jugs
onto kitchen floors.
Over spilt water, no one cries.

It is made to spill, to burst
from clotted clouds
into puddles slick with gasoline.

To strain against meniscus, its own transparent skin,
overflowing cups, sinks, rusted pipes.
To flow unbidden from the dead; plummet
from the rocky lips of rivers,
screaming whitefall.

                    Water hurtles, batters seabirds,
breaks bones, beats rock to sand. No violence rains
more reckless. Swallows robins' eggs and river rats
in its ropey muddied throat. Levels shacks
and factories where radios are made,
drowns sofas, horses, rusted Chevrolets.
Bears libraries, bar fridges, art-deco lamps
away. Acts of god.

These trials of water:
                    that it cannot hide;
even when we name it ice
or steam or snow or fog, it cannot escape.
Even though it shrinks, as a human heart shrinks
or human skin or anybody's reach;

even though at times
it seems to disappear,
water must return.
This too: water partakes of the human condition,
three-fifths. Partakes of suffering, three-fifths:
tears and perspiration, blood and spit.
Of lust, the gush of birth, the gush of sex.
Partakes of fear, drool, clammy hands,
of the heaving shame of stomachs.
The longing to be unfettered,
the common wish to be released.

NOT BY OTHER NAMES

this profusion   this stippling
after weeks and weeks of autumn rains
this rare and sudden spawning   such lush eruptions
red milky cap and yellow chanterelle
orange fairy cup and coral mushroom
pushing up into loamy undergrowth

slippery jacks and witches' butter   giant puffballs
new flesh from old corruptions
                                    a rich fungal muchness
nudging needles and blackened leaves   shoving   shouldering
the incidental earth
                        until whole pale boles appeared

on the second day we gathered shaggy manes
which grouped like tiny closed umbrellas
beside the gravel road
distinguishable only just
                                from inky cap
which should not be eaten
                            with any wine

that night my lover ate them
by herself   without Merlot

for days there were boles of scarlet waxy cap
and death cap   shiny cap and pig's ears
poison pie and snowy cap   destroying angel

the impossible places
                        where they spread
hard places   clefts and trunks of trees

tabled rocks and stumps   we'd find them there   relentless
sprouted from the moon
blue-staining boletus   the prince
the questionable stropharia
inverted brims filled with twigs and pebbles
and juvenile ferns

                                           some frilled as ears
some spread as dinner plates   some nipple-peaked
some gilled as baleen whales

days later they have vanished
gone   the angel wings and the king boletus
the blushing inocybe   all disappeared

but their names
                  diaphanous as fish tails and kaleidoscopes
fanciful as bumbershoots and silver bells   their names
remain   are spells   incantations
that mark these changelings mythic

fill the mouth with fairy sound
leave perse-blue stains

I STEEL MYSELF

if anyone asks tell them I'm sane as stainless steel
I heat the pot before I make the tea

when the Jehovah's Witnesses knock I stand
stock-still behind the drapes

I harden myself against the swords of winter rain
against December's bucket of black night

before they hatch I do not count my chickens
I boil eggs in a small tin pot

I sleep in the attic   like Dorothy I'll be first to go
Oz-bound when winds whip forty knots

I'll be the Tin Man seeking
my own heart

everyone in some small sanctuary of self is nuts
says Leo Rosten   but who knows Leo Rosten?

I don't wail   much   or rail against the price of fuel
or the cost of privacy or peace

tell them I was born this way   a tarnished spoon
between my seed-pearl baby teeth

I'm sane as any alloy   petrified as ancient wood
if they ask tell them I'm sound as an iron skillet

anything that rings hard against the knocks
holds up under heat

ON THE FERRY THROUGH ACTIVE PASS

the wings of the Bonapartes blade the sky
a skiff of snow drapes the shouldered shore

November now when things can slip away
when courses change

the gusting wind raises questions of the fractious strait
I would question you but you have gone inside

and these days like morning fog
I drift towards forgetting this place shoreline

the distant landscape leaving a lighthouse
plaintive on its blackened rock an island passing

from this perspective all the trees
                              hang from one high hill

                         until the boat's course alters
a nautical twist defying east to west bracing

against the natural arc
into the ocean's ferocious span

look back still everywhere the Bonapartes
confetti brave the waves flout the wind

THIS PARTICULAR SKY

I do not believe in God
though the sky today hangs glory
overfull and fallen
shouldering the world

white on silver   pearl grey on slate   dove grey
on gunmetal over smoke   cast shadow over tin
cloud on rounded cloud   rolling
puffed up and braided thick
as though brushed on   as though Michelangelo
lay on his scaffold and painted
this sky instead
horizon to horizon   muscled dense
claustrophobic   so near I can
almost touch it
an upside-down ocean
                    on the lip of spilling over

weighted splendour   weighted shroud
closer than I knew

EX-MOTHER-IN-LAW

We're estranged now.
She's had shingles and other afflictions
expected at her age, but she can't forgive the care
she once bestowed on me. I used to seek

her company. She told me family stories
to overcome my shyness. I was
her uncomplicated daughter; she loved me
with her whole unguarded heart.

Do you remember, dear mother-in-law:
you gave me four scallop shells
wrapped in plastic
from the cookery shop on Dunbar Street?

For your coquilles St. Jacques, you said.

The way you could expand my life.
I had never made coquilles St. Jacques
and never would.

Of the set, one bone-white shell remains,
an open hand, has found new life
as a soap dish beside my bathroom sink.

ONCE

She was sitting in the corner of the French Provincial,
the pink and grey sofa with feet that curled.
She was just sitting.
She never sat like that, looking into the middle where nothing is,
eyes swollen, hands lying in her lap.
The whole room suddenly under water.
It was the middle of the afternoon. After school.
Maybe she had finished crying.
I stopped before I reached her, not knowing.
A balled-up tissue in her hands.

Like the time, driving the I-5,
and the possum—it was on the highway's shoulder—
split open like a pomegranate, the rosy seeds.
One hundred miles an hour.
Not knowing then
what a possum looked like.
But guessing. How it caught my throat.
Not knowing a small dead animal would look like that.

That afternoon. My mother
both smaller and larger than she was.
And I ask her: what's wrong?
And she answers: nothing.
Nothing's wrong.

MY MOTHER HAD NO WINTER COAT

For years she was a snowbird. Florida.
No coat the winter her leaving was delayed
when the technician crossed her chest with blue
and laid her on the grid
                                  face down.

I sat with her in the waiting room
waiting for the radiation.
She hunched beside me in wool gloves and matching scarf;
the coat I'd bought her, too big
though I had tried it on:
same size, it should have fit.

My mother who had loved to shop for clothes,
who strode through malls as though she owned Holt Renfrew,
who loved the sun,
now sat in a winter coat she hadn't bought
with sleeves that hid her fingertips.

Nothing fit that year. Not the coat, not the latitude,
nor her breath inside her lungs.

THE LAST TIME I SPOKE TO HER

my sister's voice saying *she's conscious now* the phone heavy in my right hand and my mother's voice faint and me saying *Mum* as though saying her name could bring her close then my name *Arleen* her voice so thin *how do you take your porridge? with brown sugar* I answer but wrong the most important question I will ever answer and I'm wrong *one spoonful no* she's saying *no not sugar* a quiz morphine-fuelled maybe she's asking about my father who takes his porridge with a half teaspoonful of salt *salt is it salt?* but *no* she says *not salt*

then my sister's voice saying to me *goodbye* my mother tired and gone with no right answer and I am left on my blue sofa gold threads and ivory stripes white shag under my feet and the day a weekend day eleven-fifteen kids still eating pancakes in the kitchen and I cannot lift myself from the cushioned seat my left hand tracing retracing one too-smooth ivory stripe my right hand tight round the black receiver

AS CLOSE TO WATER'S EDGE

Let your eyes survey tall grasses: eel, sword, sedge,
a calculation of grey-green and ochred culms,
flat stemmed, triangulate, ribbed,
some blades as sharp as boning knives—
the way the hawk perceives
opportunity
among the moving stalks.

Your feet runnel swaths down to the waves,
rounded rocks, caves beyond blurred edges.
Driftwood jammed up, bull-kelp bulbs,
whips, rosehips, dead twigs,
glass, bits of ship, seaweed maps
iridescent in slant sun.

Your feet are not steady but hold ground.
Their grip rooting under pebbled rock.

Your mind metes out judgments
the way salt measures time.
Questions about the debris rise like tides
and fall away. Volumes of unknowing
lap the wall, broken and gapped, built
to divide the grasses from the beach,
white irises and wild willow foam.
Do not compare. Be still. Be
everything that washes up on shore.

IN NOMINE DUST

Unwrap the dust from its mummy cloths.
                    —Denise Levertov

Breathe it, commit it to memory,
dust, its genus, its everyday and its other names too.
Cinders and sand, hair, crusts of bread
all collapse in one direction. Conjugate dust's provenance,
particulates, formal and vernacular, everlasting.
De moleculorum. Cosmologies of dust, religions, philosophies:
all list that way. Names written on earth.
Omega dust and alpha, dust freed
from tombstones and tabletops
from seed pods wilding on wind.
In jubilation. Evidence of what remains.

Interstellar, but born also of city soot
and the discarded skins of snakes.
Tracked in bands of sunlight, adagio,
murmurous motes shining gloriosa
through morning slats.

Collect its human names, in particular, the dying and the dead,
its given names:
Adelaide and Celestine, for example,
Felix and Seraphim in the cemetery in Dorval
where I grew up. Each name falling from the bone.
As in graveyards in Moose Jaw and in Salt Lake City
in mausoleums, crematoria, in tombs on the Nile.

Memorize them, found and multitudinous:
they are the the names of dust.
In Notre Dame in Ottawa where my father rests
the dust there is known as James and as Agnes,

Lazar, Thomas, Marie-Blanche.
In the same way, the firmament, gold dust,
light years, dust of thunder clouds
dust under camel hooves, under basement stairs,
in the vaults of old banks, catacombs, the dust of self.
Dust to dust, endless, even in this,
the poem's amplifying chamber, endlessness
having entered time and all these words.

Know it in its aggregations, in calm
for the peace it brings. And

in malevolence, for its harm:
                              dust bowls for instance,
the term for prairie storms, pulvis infidelis,
the swirl of weary earth fleeing without escape,
filling plates set out for dry-eyed children,
sacramentis, their mouths filled
with its profane
name, its everyday, their teeth,
their hair packed with it.
Their elders choking.
                    Its daily whine
against the children's narrow shins.

Know it as it forms the nucleus
of raindrops, centralis, innocent,
first grace note of snow.

                    It forms the core
of our becoming, separate and in chorus.
In gratitude. The cradle, coffin, us and them
and dust. The long decay, prolonged from early days;

the coming apart of ordinary bodies ending
as they start. Insects and epidermis,
this dry, soft, downy desiccation
into future.
All names are dust, farfetched, formal, everyday. Incantations.
I include my own. And the names of my children.

Coming apart under the speckled sky.
We are cradles, graves, floating
this froth of stars. Thinking ourselves whole
but knowing
ourselves particulate,
in pax vobiscum, essential grit.

FALL IN THE BACKYARD

The garden nods. A new sky overhead.
The petals of the Karma dahlia reach

for their salvation. The lettuce heads are bolting
in revolt, while evening primrose hangs

its blooms, pale, crestfallen, as though jilted by summer.
Nothing can revive them. Overhead the sky turns from rain

to electric blue. Dark as blood blisters, the little apples
hold fiercely to their tree. No one knows

their name. Like children who overstay childhood,
they resist, sweeten late.

Sunlight settles half the yard, the rest remains
in wistfulness, dark earth. The wind blows,

reproves, tugs fruit, ruffles grass, warns each petal dying:
light and shadow both—nothing holds forever.

PREPARING THE WAY, SHE CUTS THE PERCHES
FROM THE HUMMINGBIRD FEEDER

She wants them, their ruby gorgets, emerald backs, fast as light.
She wants them
to want her, to land on her finger outstretched.

She cuts the perch, places the feeder
above her head, above the place where she sleeps
every night on her porch.
When she wakes, she holds out her finger
under the feeder. Infinite patience. Weeks of it, every day,
every night sleeping in the domed hollow of stars,
the risk that rests on her cheek—waiting.

Then it happens. One bird,
she knows it by heart—lands. One bird.
The clench of its miniscule claws.

She is a trick, a soft platform to feed from, a perch made of flesh.

But O—
            when the way is prepared, who is not seduced?
Blameless, we want what we want:
                        sweetness, a safe place to land.

MAN FROM ANOTHER COUNTRY

Thinking on that man from another country, another century,
my grandfather, fathered in Antrim, unfathered
in a barn by a mother unwed, unfamilied there,
the two farms already too divided for marriage.

Unschooled, a Heathcliff—work then, farmhand,
the farmland growing his shoulders broad as two yokes
and his hands the size of two hams.
The way he could handle a horse in a field, pitch the hay.

The way from that place, always unwanted,
he crossed the water—through the years, growing a family—
Glasgow, the yards on the Clyde—
to handle sheets of hot steel hand over hand
off the press; flask of whiskey fisted for his lunch
the whistles for breaks, short, beginning to end.
                                        And yet,
what is known as work is its own consolation.
Then becoming unworked—the 1920s—the years the yards closed—
unwanted again. Thinking of him crossing new water,
and no longer young, unable to find any work

except to walk out in the morning onto the water,
frozen and whitened with snow,
that lay under the rapids of the old canal in Lachine—
coatless and hatless, now fifty-nine—

to chop blocks of ice every day until spring.

YOU DIED UNSURROUNDED

Your last day alive was the day
                      I meant to call—
three thousand miles—before I left for the office—but—

the sink, and the drain filled with coffee grinds,
the plumber arrived early, rush-hour traffic
and the phone rates those days
                      were best before eight.

You waited all morning, your second wife said, for my call
(though even she wasn't there),
reading the paper front page to last, watching the trees
from the hospital window—in new yellow leaf.

Your lungs, unreliable, and your daughters unreliable too.
And so, grasping the implications,
you folded the paper in half and in half again,
smoothed the crease,
                   placed it at the foot of the bed,
while you rucked in one breath at a time,
the arc of each inhalation
descending
               to nothing
dying in a blue cotton gown,
unsurrounded, unseen.

HE LEAVES HIS FACE IN THE FUNERAL CAR

Back seat of the funeral car, our father's second wife tells me
I should've called.

Her four daughters, whom I hardly know, avert their eyes.
My own sister sits beside me, shoulders squared, while our father

leads in the hearse ahead through this curse of afternoon traffic
to his own cremation.

My mouth is set, a steel handle on an old dresser drawer.
My face, which is my father's,

glides windowed by, given back against the passing leaves,
feathered bitter, feathered sweet, this time of year. My father

leading us, leaves. Leaves his money in three awkward thirds. Leaves
my girlfriend his tuxedo pants. Leaves

his *Jesus Murphy* and his *hell's bells* along with his joke
about Paddy O'Furniture, which no one found funny.

And his rage, which I claim, he also leaves, and his tie rack,
inlaid with red and black squares.

His face too, he wills me for as long as I need—
his tempered jaw, his burnt blue eyes.

VIS-À-VIS CLOCKS

the wind outside grows furious with the trees
the rain relentless
I rush about the house as if I had

somewhere to go   the hydro wires rock
devoid of birds
the rain reneges

and still I rush about
in and out of rooms
I have no dog or cat

to comfort me and despite
prevailing risk
I carry no canary on my wrist

what matters is my grip on things
and knowing when
to call a halt

I have never learned
to arrange myself
vis-à-vis the clocks

though I study their faces
watch their hands
claw past every number

ARBUTUS IN THE SWEET-LIGHT

shadows lace the sun-spangled leaves
this arbutus
        curving ruddy
        curving out far over the cliffside
towards something
        just out of reach unseen

what is untouchable my longing intangible
the tree's chartreuse underskin
its basketries of orange light deep-dazzle
breeze-shaped the tree's berries
          red bells bunched
in this evening's sweet-light saturation

each leaf lacquered the tree almost a torch
backdropped against blue teal the ocean
its own lancing lights

        if addressed
would it know its true name
this tree
      which is desire

would it know its provenance
      which is beauty

this flammable mercy
infinite unbearable cleave

FOR THE GARRY OAK IN SPRING

you spiral spill fork twist
your grey encrypted trunk
corkscrew tips
your branches ankylosing whipped
wrong turns and rights misses
and mistakes preconditions of your wit

two California quail
in silt and black with curling tops
quill your limbs
the whole fills up criss-crossing blue
brimming
              while the quail step down your blistered bark
gather for teachings

what lifts you leads you
each branch's bend buckled against the one before
                                    inside your spacious net

such precision following less the light
than your unresisted will your art
your gibbous maze of soul

at the end of every branch a fistlet
about to burst its velvet glove

INTERIOR: A BRIEF HISTORY OF LANDSCAPE

After Maryl McMaster's Sentience,
In-Between Worlds series, 2010, digital chromogenic print

Feathers and twigs are here. And hands. The way the two hands.
The image composed, compelling.
The way they criss-cross in clasp on the face of this tree in caress,
this blooded, black-barked, wet-necked, fissured tree—
captured, embraced.
Human heart is here, hidden,
buckled far side against the scabrous trunk. Who cares for whom?
Does the tree?
And to what are the elbows attached?
What are the birds? Their rufus brown feathers and grey,
brown thrasher, thrush, house sparrow or song?
The soft downies of barred owls or small sharp-shinned hawks?
Everything is bare. Except feathers
glued to the forearms like sleeves, adornments of wings.
Beauty too. Bare. Except twigs bound to the backs of fingers,
taloned, with small twists of wire. Haywire.
A crescent of shoulder is here. But not clothes. Clothes are missing.
Face too. The trunk is a mask. Tree mask or bark? How many disguises?
How many birds die every day?
The tree is tipped slightly east, slightly right. What isn't?
Everywhere snow and black holes for the trees drifting into the past.
In truth, there is only one tree. In truth
the difference between tree and bird, between bird
and two human hands,
is one of degree. Not kind. Her hands turn pellucid in transformation.
Who here is stranded? What is strange, strangled?
Who beloved? Immersed, almost lost.

II

VENICE

from the airport you can approach this drowning city
by the sea bus Alilaguna
the city's salt   its foam   its outer waters slapping the flat sides
of this flat-bottomed boat   approaching
history
             which sinks   plaster and marble   celadon blue
the boat's engines chugging   archangels
singing beneath the old boards

wind snaps   your head cants from the boat's open window
hair streaming   keening into cool blue air

the skyline ripples with domes   steeples   painted-on stars

through this Laguna   water rising   while history recedes
the wide narrows   the boat's engines gear down
swells change to chop   the blow to breeze

wisteria   mimosa   banners and bunting   window boxes
cascading yellow lacing over stone walls

you are the first
                 unjaded   as every traveller is
the newest eye   nothing
                          disappoints   nothing spoils
you chug past the island of the cemeteria
and Burano   San Marco   the Grand Canal
trees waving even as they thin out to none
bridges hunch their narrow backs   gold leaf and green mosaics
splay the old facades
shutters close over windows   doors   shadows
stretch out exhausted

plaster walls paint themselves with the sun setting
all the while   the city's buildings filling up with salt—
you have arrived

BORDER CROSSING AT ALDERGROVE

we watch the endless bumpered line of stopping
starting stopping
                  cars
                  inch along the Interstate
the drivers glazing over gazing over
the levelled but still unlevel land
the farms their undulations their rivered fields of summer singing
heedless of the traffic choke
                  the longest border undefended
but always with drug dogs and side arms at the ready

beyond the highway's vistas rural roads
the rounded rolled-out hubris
swells and breaks into squared and proper lines
hedgerows guard the corn fields the white silk

legal boundaries and boundaries that are deciduous
assembled fences
one country ends another begins

the Itzakadoozie ice-cream truck is blue
bright as opportunity
its do-dah do-dah music
                  clear as unclouded skies
unbounded unlimned

MEMORIAL ON THE BOULEVARD

this dead boy   hair thick
blond as the Milky Way
Arcadian   his high school beauty gowned
pink-cheeked in his graduation photo

framed this way
                          he guards the intersection
of Hemlock and King   his eyes
this morning hide   obscured
by orange and yellow asters
jam-jarred salal and pale phlox floribunda

his mouth smiles at cars as they speed past
and above his shoulders
a painted mauve sky

he has a mother
she comes most days to visit him

does she avert her eyes as she rubs road grit
from the glass?   as she places asters
round his bright face?

it's been three years   her grief
measured now in jars
                          and broken stems.

ODE TO HAZEL WHITE

Her name, I finally learned,
the Sunday morning she was buried,
was Hazel White.
Referred to simply in earlier reports as
    a family friend just dropping by.

Shot in the back, killed in a northern town
by a husband not her own. Bad luck,
dropping by when the ex comes round
with his shotgun—how it was reported
all that week on CBC: friend, dropping by, shot.
All week I puzzled at the happenstance.
Was she sitting at the kitchen table having tea
when he decided
                to shoot her instead?

                Then, early Sunday morning radio
reported her funeral: how she stood that day
with a plank in her white-knuckled hands
against the man with the gun outside the cabin
where her friend lived with two daughters.

Hazel White warned him: *You won't get her
unless you get by me.* That's what she said.

When he advanced
she swung,
             missed.

He shot her then, as she wheeled around,
between the shoulder blades.

CRISIS LINE AT 2 A.M.

I'm calling about this friend, who's my age—fifteen—he's in trouble. These grade twelve guys—my dad calls them the four horsemen—they've got jackets with skulls. They chase him, see, shouting like they're gonna tear off his arms. They call him fag. He gets this funny taste in his mouth—like ashes. They call him bitch. Some mornings he vomits up his breakfast.
My dad says.... I found this number in the phone book. It's always after school, so my friend has to leave school early. My dad says if he *is* a faggot.... They know his house. My friend's going to get his uncle's .22—at least that's what he says. Sit in the field back of the church, put the barrel in his mouth.... He's got no friends, see.

Are you still there?

DREAM OF A BULLET

you were dancing—the woman tells me
she saw me from her window
singing to myself

she's not a friend of mine   I don't even know her last name
apparently I just happened to be in her backyard
in the dream
my mouth   my two feet moving   when a bullet
she says
pierced my throat   blood gurgling up

she ran to save me   held my neck
                             emptied now of song
my blood staining her arm

the improbable angle of the bullet
when it entered
                       she says
kneeling over me the way Jackie
draped herself over Jack
back seat of the limousine

it was not my fault   she says
I did not pull the trigger

WINTER SOLSTICE: TURNING POINT

This time of year the minutes fall
one by nacred one from the ends of days,

beads of rain collect,
dropping from leftover leaves.

The crows hunch, huddled
in the pear tree's blackened branches.

I try to stay inside my body, craving warmth
and whatever foils the endless dark,

whatever calms the storms that fissure sidewalks,
split fruit still stitched to trees.

Twelve candles. A flaming hearth. Forty days
of incandescent light.

Like the crows, throats gurgled with rain, I watch,
one ear to the heavens, listening

for the shift, for the sun, us, the streets, the Earth,
                                        to turn, to tilt.

MASSETT MUSEUM—1990

the museum is quiet today
outside   no one walks the road
no cars no bicycles raise yellow dust
no dogs lie on the verge

in the room
there is only one room
there is a map   hung between the photographs
hand-drawn
it shows where the people
in their thousands   in their
tens of thousands
once lived   for ten thousand years
a tracery of small yellow pins   numerous as stars
marks villages   trade routes   commerce
where canoes
navigated the long curve of coast

the map so lived on
                    that once you see it
you cannot not

showing the time before
before
measles and typhoid   scarlet fever
chicken pox and diphtheria
the time before smallpox
tucked into woollen blankets

which left longhouses
                              empty
and canoes to list on the shore

and the carved poles in the forests
to fall into sky

FOR THE RECORD

Anna Probyn, 16, escapes father's hands through Admissions door of Essondale, stays on locked ward sixty years. Forgets every word she ever learned.

Claudia Clyde, 32, leaves a downtown hotel through a seventh-storey window, leaves three haranguing voices in the room. Her legs on the sidewalk.

Shirley Oaten, 47, crosses First Avenue against the red light, looking straight ahead, handbag in hand, transistor radio somewhere at the bottom. Three lanes of traffic, fingertips burnt orange. Makes it to the middle.

For the record: Anna's handshake was a silken flag.

Sandra Baxter, 29, places herself on her boyfriend's sofa, switches on electric carving knife, holds it hard against her throat. Boyfriend out for a pack of cigarettes, a bag of taco chips.

Paul Needham, 23, crosses two highways—Riverview to Port Mann Bridge—leaves Port Mann Bridge at the upper crest, drops thirty storeys. Water like cement.

Shirley strode through time like a northern elk. Her brother did not attend the service.

Paul Needham, sweet-faced, moved through wards like the Paraclete.

Jane Poole, 35, refuses food, loses hair, refuses friends, loses teeth, loses kidney function. Loses heart.

For the record, unofficial: everyone lost heart.

HER NAME WAS ANNA AND YOU SHOULD KNOW

That she shook my hand, having just been introduced and
this social-work ritual so foreign to her;
that she tried to smile though shy as a mole, having no reason to trust,
her handshake thin, soft, an old kidskin glove.

That she stood in house slippers midday and wore a cotton housedress
that zipped up the front, though she lived in no house.
That the doctors said she was ready for discharge,
that she had stayed sixty years in this place.
That she no longer spoke.

That the walls in the halls of this hospital were hospital green
and all the doors were locked at all times.
That the orderlies wore keys round their belts, so many, they sounded
like bells.
The opening and closing of locks day and night.

That she slept in the same dormitory room for sixty years
with the same forty beds lined in the same measured rows.

That the TV could leer, could observe, oversized and high cornered
in the common room where forty patients sat in folding chairs
placed around the four walls,
or paced in straight lines or in circles,
sometimes crying out.

You should know that her mother died when she was sixteen.
That they brought her here to this place, same year, looking twelve
with her Buster Brown hair in the small black and white
taped to the cover of her thick patient file.

That she was just a girl that spring day in 1921,
smiling for the camera,

despite her mother's death, despite the stone buildings and the tall wooden doors,
despite
     the primary reason the doctors listed that day
for her admission: *that she had allowed her father*
          to molest her.

You should know
that this story is true.

THE NEIGHBOUR

Once a narrow creek
wound behind Mrs. Paul's house.
Milkweed in spring, burrs in the fall.
Once my sister bit into her wrist.
In those days, the women stayed home.
They owned knives and aluminum pots.
Her husband once sold aluminum doors.
Dogs died. Once a cat was found
after six months of winter at the entrance to a culvert,
brick-stiff.

Mrs. Paul sits in a green velvet armchair
slightly turned away from her living-room window.
She knows who passes by,
when each tree drops its leaves,
whose car, ten years ago, drove into the telephone pole.
A book rests in her hands.

It's late March. In small islets, snow disappears
into the grass.
She is heroic and the snow this year
is late to leave.

LONG DISTANCE

my sister lives three thousand miles to the east   the distance
shocking   in her house   does she sit by her phone?

as a child she slept in a twin bed three feet from mine
together we breathed the same furnace-forced air

once she told me I was her other mother   for years
we've hoped to share bowls of soup in our kitchens
at least once a week

between pencil and page   first letter   last   telephone
fibre optics   the impossible gap   nothing

close enough   breaches   apertures inside
the part of the mind that shelters

the heart   we are altered   I sit here beside my own phone
tap my keyboard
three thousand miles to the west

MY SISTER SITS

                       at the mirror
watching her hair turn white.
she's been sitting there for days

for years she dyed her hair
a shade of red called
Old Flame   sixty now   tired

of dyeing   beyond all that
liz taylor   cher
nancy reagan   jane

fonda   the magazines tell her she must
stop the clock   stay young   eat greens   sleep   run
nip   tuck   dye

pluck
eyebrows and small hairs that crowd round the mouth
wear it short   smile   don't smile too much

watches
her mouth   the tented corners
near her eyes

counts each new line   squints
waits   the way she first awaited
her adolescent breasts

buds quickening   unfamiliar
she knew then   life passing
the sure approach of the end

CONVERSATION ON MONDAY MORNING

my friend Heather is growing deaf
when she asks me to repeat
what I said about house sparrows
and the nests of winter wrens
she smiles
as though her deafness is a riddle

something she almost can
solve.

IRRECONCILABLE SUMMER

summer arrived late
                    last evening
into the reaches of firs
tipped orange
                    sun slipping
beneath the broad bands of cloud
burnished ribbons   hemlock needles turned copper
kinglets wrens

but this morning again drizzle crazes the panes
again a wood fire swells the hearth
I keep it company
needlework while the sun snubs the beach grass
the sun's position shrouded once more

the long pall of afternoon stretches grey
into grey
spends itself in nimbus and apparitions

when I was twelve
that summer too failed to find us
we did not move to the cottage   instead
we played crazy eights solitaire old maid
on the dining-room table in town
I did not know what to long for

since then the camellia has grown up past the window
its leaves fringe the old rivered glass
restless again with the rain

MRS. BOOTH'S NEW BABY BEETS

sure I cook sew too newfangled holer embroiderer the works but
it's my beets Stan loves my pickled beets he can't get enough and now
this second crop who has a second crop this time of year course my
curly fries I make curly fries like who-ever-it-was made the *Mona Lisa*
and not that I want to blow my own horn but that hunting sweater size
large only seven days roll collar three ducks on the back flying like
they just heard a canon for young Stan

                        comes over last night with Debbie the two
girls 'specting dinner half dozen mallards hanging beak-down from his
hands *hang 'em up Ma* and who's s'posed to pluck gut dress pack and
stuff 'em into plastic bags beaks dripping on the floor like my kitchen's
an abattoir I hooked 'em over the coat rack I like duck but I don't really
love it

I'm out of the room one minute and they're at it Stan and Stan shout-
ing who needs two Stans all the thanks I get I got neighbours I got
feelings I cook I sew upholster sofas and chairs my garden rivals the
farmer's in the dell I make gravy you could serve to the queen jars of
pickled beets babies same size as duck hearts but sweet

MEDITATION AT WESTWOOD LAKE

is silence six days waking at five forty-five   walking like learning to walk watching alder leaves riff the air   watching sparrows nibble the old sidewalk cement from parking lot to hall where we sit pine needles crusting the path   heads looking down sitting apart shawls on our laps breathing noting the breath hands rooting in place lake through the windows the quicksilver water some aspect of lake surface moving with ghosts herringbone light weaving black-water shadows the lake in this place west coast artificial   leaving tall trees knee-deep in water dead   a red-eyed towhee busies the top of the hand-carved varnished sign no god no angels starting again breathing watching the breath the pinprick of black in the towhee's bright eye   stands of lake-flooded trees stranded   beheaded trunks reach like flagpoles into the clouds.

MOONRIND

I rift from the night, a paring. At thought's edge
a new moon sickles its bearings.

Late lunar intention. This question of loyalties.
I don't ask for much, but I don't trust much either.

Can entrails tipped onto stone interpret a life?
A coin flipped, the peel of a golden delicious spell out

the new lover's name? Insidious hurt. If I look the other way
it's not there at all. The moon losing face.

Leaving the restaurant, we flip up our collars,
despite the spring tulips guarding the street.

My hunger's a barrel. In my chest I wear a bitter crest
somewhere between full rose and wolf moon.

We ate white fish; we drank white wine.

Who knows the provenance of hurt?
Another woman's eyes, their trajectory determined.

Your body. When I leave you at the corner
I kiss you. The risk tonight of leaving at all. Familiar cold

rising, gathering its mane from the grass. The moon
so slender, a pike on the turn.

NINE REASONS TO PREFER THE PEAR

i
a single longing   tear-dropped
from its stem   almost
lost in yellow leaves

ii
three upright in a bowl
the bowl is blue   the air slowing
as though they were breathing

iii
paired on a plate
their blushing skins side by side
for company   two knives

iv
mothers-in-law prefer pears
to plums   such snobs
but they know their fruit

v
more than six is too many
unless they're poached in wine
in wine no number is too many

vi
a pear is not hurried   a pear
is not fooled   unlike an orange
a pear knows which end is up

vii
pears hide their stone cells close to their core
a cool gravitas   in water apples float
pears swoon beneath

viii
pears belong in porcelain   as do tulips
bananas belong in lunch bags
pears on purple silk

ix
when an apple's offered   it comes with caveats
when a pear is offered   red bartlett
anjou forelle   can love be far behind?

SHE ASKED FOR BIRDS

For Kelly Parsons, the poet who asked for birds
—after an untitled painting by Carl Hessay

when the birds arrive they land in inky trees
stud the forest
        already full of abstract life   though life
is not what this is about
and the birds knowing nothing of the poet's final request
sleep through the night
as though they've arrived on the far side of flight
all species
        as if there might be another flood

in the morning they can't lift their twig feet
from around the black boughs
growing into this place
spanish moss sunset broken limbs
the wild entanglements
that a painter's mind and sufficient pigment can make

their colours bleed blending
becoming part of

        the forest becoming the birds
bark attaching itself to the undersides of wings
the insides of feather struts
birds calling to the future and the future
        knowing little of origins

presents itself in cataclysmic time
everything moving too fast or not at all
but merging
        the way the poet died
into the lives of those around her

MEMORIAL SERVICE

The infant in the front row—her head a kewpie doll's head—
wears the face of the dead woman,
her grandmother, the poet,
who once asked for birds.

The child's cheeks are paradise puddings.
The silk of her mother's sleeve lies loose on her lips.

It's hard to know what to choose—after-life
or life-after-life-after-life. Or nothing at all.
The dead woman gone, gone beyond.

It's tempting to think the child might have answers,
something to say about beginnings
and ends,
as though she had unfolded sonnets
and syllogisms
not long before her recent birth
or listed the Latin names
of ravens, larks, maybe hawks. Clearly

she listens to only half of what the priest says.

And no one can advise the child about the face she is heir to,
or where the woman who once owned it has gone.

No one really expects the child to pass on what she'd learned
from her past. She can't speak.
She could sleep; instead she studies the leaves
on the sleeve of her mother's black and white dress.

CITY SLANTS

After an untitled painting by Carl Hessay

the city expands   morning sun cuts lucid as truth
through the broad Venetian slats.

bands of mauve and ochre light
indicate the place of sparrow song
the value of brushes and oils
white-crowned and vesper

the high-rise concrete walls
meet the sidewalk in cavernous shadow
in the loneliness of first violins

art serves
to calm the random worries
of the metropolis   uplifts   disguises what might distress

horizontal bands signify states of rest
a lost boot   broken glass   feral cats   the shape of the city
free this morning from pity or shame

OLD AT FORTY-EIGHT...

After the portrait of Hille Bobbe by Frans Hals

...or is she only thirty-six, prematurely worn,
her hair not yet grey beneath her brimless bonnet.

Maybe it's the mauve rose smearing her cheeks,
or her oily brow, puckered with paint, that weathers her.

Or do her teeth betray, blunt, numbered
in her slant rakish mouth. She could be

laughing but what would be humorous
in this pub on this night: the fog, the war,
this Frans Hals, gin-sodden,
slipping in his own turpentine?

That he supposes he paints her likeness—who she really is—
might be laughable. She no longer knows
how her days can move the way they do,
sliding only into the past—
where her four sons are buried.

Her dress is slick with the passage of time,
her soiled ruff hangs short fingers round her short neck.
The years have moved her beyond the burdens of she or he—
not yet angel or spirit—
have moved her beyond what's approved,

and yet this night, the tankard she holds in her hand
glimmers as the full moon. She is her own sun.
And the owl that tilts on her shoulder,
otherworldly, denies that the world knows what it sees.

SOME BLUE IS STONE

stones can be divided   sorted   stones
can be heavy as a dead man's dead hand
or light as June rain chiming into old backyard barrels

stones can be curved as robins' eggs
smooth or vaguely hived
or hatched
                              emptied out
round as plums blued with bloom

there are mountains in the west that pierce the sky
where glacial lakes hide

early mountaineers wore worsted wool
at higher elevations their fingers froze
they carried compasses in their pockets
wore tins of water hitched to their belts
coils of rope round their shoulders and necks

they named the peaks   each name dividing

mountains from ranges and mountains
from mountains Ringrose from Temple Cathedral
from Hungabee   divided lakes from lakes   Oesa
from O'Hara   Mary from MacArthur
Louise from Lefroy

pickaxes by their sides
by the sides of tarns tinted with plumes of fine silt
salted with cold
they divided mountaintops from the mountain-tipped sky

colour's a spectrum   visible   divisible
blue   is a stone that fits into the palm
is rosemary   bergamot   snow

ON BALANCE

The Great Blondin walked across Niagara Falls
more than twelve times on a rope no thicker than his upper arm,
once with his agent on his back.

Which begs the question: why?
For money or meaning? Fame? Something to do?
Once, midway, he scrambled six eggs.

The question why is a hook, baited with hope.
Or despair.
Who doesn't ask it? Who doesn't hazard a guess?

There are more ways to fall than to left or to right—
into cataract or void—
at least three hundred and fifty-eight.

In 1932 the Falls froze solid; anyone with cleated boots
could pick their way across.

UNGULATE WITHIN

Nodding yes, yes,
I drive past banks of clover
and grasses with plumy heads,
mauve and avocado-coloured stalks.
Yes, in the light evening breeze.

They make me happy.
I must be hungry.
Maybe I am not
what I think I am.

Maybe I am
a deer driving a car
with the windows rolled down,
heading home,
taste of dinner,
grasses and clover, sweet
between my ruminant teeth.

THE NEXT MORNING, THE TEA KETTLE'S A SIEVE

They had been warned against leaving—
gunshots or growling—to stay in their rooms,
their mother said,
before she left in the car for a meeting in town.
The girl sat in the bedroom with her older sister, too early for sleep,
their two little brothers in bed down the hall. The hall light
watching over them all.
Do not go downstairs, their mother had said, nothing is safe down the stairs.
And then
                    gunshots—again and again—in the kitchen the sound
of pots falling. Their father. Drunk. Wanting noise
in the pots, noise in the soup bowls, cups, the white saucers
with the small yellow roses. The girl could hear the small roses
explode. A black wind hard on the window, hard
in the trees in the backyard, boats cascading high waves, cat-o'-nine-tails.
Inside the frame, the fine rattle of bones.
And still her sister sat on the bed, not moving, head
cocked to one side, not saying a word.

AUBADE FOR AN UNDERGROUND RIVER

beyond this speck-spit windshield   north-end port near the ocean's
industrial edge   the man makes his way where the city tilts into inlet
where commerce rumbles beyond the rail yards   chain-link billboards
battered hotels   a car wash a marine-supply outlet   a rendering plant
a sandwich shop boarded up   the man lurches alone eastbound at this
dull start-of-day midweek a work day his ambulation uncertain as a
broken pump   through this underbelly   wearing the same clothes he
wore the day before this man listing reckless conversing with the half-
light   and me on my way to the office waiting for the long red to turn
both of us predictable as rain in November

no other cars on the road   sidewalk empty but for him his
legs bandied and bent   his broken shoes   his lips moving walking his
way in the other direction   we meet   not meeting   weekdays just after
dawn   the open air clanging   free   ions negative and cold   a lament
quiet as an underground creek a river running buried under this street.

WHEN THERE WERE BEES, INCESSANT HUMMING

bees once broidered the old plum over-brimmed as it was every April
fat blossoms white smears and pale pink two decades ago those days
the tree was a festival a phantasmagorical bedazzle spilling Milky Way
sounds out into the spin somewhere into the poorly lit past or the future
the universe we call Andromeda and I in love with the bees' murmu-
rations the bees and I in love with the tree the breeze lifting string
sound vibrations the tree lifting out of itself out of bark and newly
born leaves the clear unstoppable bombilate *omm* the plenitudinous
tremble leftover grass prodding its roots the plum having survived
another long winter of rain finally bedizened with bees honey or bum-
ble humming telling each other

      that was years ago zithers or violins played in a well a high-level
swell the pitch a warning the branches listening like bendable pencils
taking dictation

      taking all of it down

bees and the tree and the hum into blue everlasting everything lasting
year after year until

      the bees one year

      are almost gone colonies collapsed ghost wings iridescent
they say with toxins and virus

      everything changing all shifted lifted out of itself out of
life seasons off the wheel the plum too toppled everything no
longer there

SEQUENCE FOR A YOUNGER SON

January dawn: streetlights silver the sifting snow.
I read at an angle, an excerpt from *Deliverance*:
mountain men and shotguns.
This infant in my arms.
Twenty watts shed only so much light.
The armchair with arms flat enough to balance anything.
I look across the page, the river:
on the far side, a bottle,
some kind of formula.

~

From the bathroom the summer you were almost two
you call my name, Mum, stay with me, you say,
it's plain in here without you.

~

Every evening sun leaves the sky, vacates the house-lined street;
books and voices, telephones recede. God left long ago.
How fixed the weight of night. How distant each horizon.

~

In early fall, crabapples loosen from the backyard tree.
Against the whitewashed wall.

~

Not every script reads left to right.
Not every fish wears scales. Some doors open left.
A firefly's light is not reflected light, nor is it incandescent:
it shines luciferin. Summer evenings,

as many children as those grassy stars.
Each child holds a mason jar; each jar bears a lid.

~

Years ago, butterflies covered every blade,
the grass thick with buckeyes, ursulas, monarchs, lunar moths.
The flutter, flight, the quiver, life alight.
Years ago.

~

Eremiophobia means I always want you near.
The impossibility of left, of leaving.
I lie in the belly of a dream,
leap from the hold of a high-flying plane.
Wend the surface of an east-flowing river.
Fall through floorboards. Open
my mouth, expecting rain. I fall
through. I rise. Wait for you.
Wait for the rain to come.

FIRE

in the beginning was fire
not water   not stone   not rosy finches or breath
flat worms or primordial slime   but fire

the unsolvable void   gaseous
scarlet letters   Arabic script   blue and orange blaze
explosive cosmic sharp-scented heat
infinitude   trails   tongues   tails
all things inflammable

when we say starry night   we mean fire
when we say sun   fire   we mean billowing
when we say hearth   we mean home

my son slept in the basement deep as a wintering bear
he was seventeen   so
when the house caught fire in April   he didn't
wake   could not be roused
his father carried him out in his arms
through flames and smoke thick as London's old fogs

what if
don't say   what if

when we say alarm   house   fire   barn   horses   oil fields   forests
underground root systems on the ridge above Jarvis Inlet
irrepressible   consecutive summers catching again and again
black timbers   black bones

when we say first causes   we mean spark
belly   headlong
we say heart   mean love

the all-combustible word swelling
away from itself we mean everlasting

the difference between fire and stone
is a handful of sand
the difference between fire and flesh
the difference
                    my son carried out
between fire and flesh

FIRE THORN

The pyracantha grows along the front deck
a foot above the wood rail. Beyond that,
the new cedar fence. Beyond that,
the cove, in roil today, shook foil,
sun shining through conifers to the northwest.

But the pyracantha,
                  its structure dense, a wall, green leaf and berries
lacquered orange Chinese red, tight-fisted bouquets.
The leaves are serrated, smaller than a pine siskin's wing.
The berries, pomes, poisonous, unclappered bells—not poisonous
for particular birds. Yesterday four varied thrush,
bright orange and gold, gorged, diving deep—heedless
of fire thorns, fine spires—into the bush. But today,
the muted-brown robin drove a thrush into our pane.
                        That soft thud on the glass.

In the middle where the robin now sits, stout queen,
nestled low in a nest of sharp-sided growth,
there, most berries are gone.

Last spring, a pair of mallards swam close to the shore,
the male green-feathered and blue. Seeing them
for the first time, my young grandson said
he preferred the female
fiercer
in her dull streaky greys.

ECHO CARDIOGRAM

I saw
my heart
last week
onscreen
real time
saw two
small leaf-
like valves
fling-wide
ca-close
fling-wide

non-stop
no rest

I loved
the beat
three-quar-
ter song
all on
its own
without
me to
turn it
on or

monarch
wings   crick-
et leap
ruby-
crowned bird
something
so wild

and I
grateful
for this
intre-
pid heart
more loyal
than my
own mind

      I
would have
knelt to
it —
     but
I was
wired down

BLACK EAGLES

Black eagles fester the view
outside my aunt's second-floor nursing-home window.
They pick off the small browns, pluck
featherless nestlings
from nests in the trees, menace robins,
grey squirrels splayed on the trunks.
Their wingspan so brooding
broad, they buckle branches, block out
whole pieces of sky. See
what the biggest one carries away in its mouth,
she says.
I nod,
            but I don't.

How can I
                deny her black eagles?
Wraiths.
The view from the window is all she has left.

How can I not see
what the black eagles carry away.

EVEN ON DAYS WHEN THE SKY IS NOT BLUE

how far they come   the swallows   how far
they go   aiming cumulus to horsetail
how high   how cold the air

how seagulls and geese drown the sky
                              rival city streets
with the spangled sounds of clowns
or bellow's noise
                    or the ring of rusted hinges

birds   the sheer physics of flight
how the sight of them can fill us
with blessings

how they simply do not die up there
but dominate the wind
rearrange the sun's light

the robins so early   piping in days
remaining less certain
when nighttime begins

how doves balance among the needles of ponderosa pine
or on rooftops
or hydro wires thin as rails of rain

how the heron can meditate for hours
on one fine twig of leg

how fast crows break the laws
of gravity for instance

the swallow   the hawk
innocent
not meaning what we make them mean

how they convince us of ecstasy
of escape from worn-out ways
so even the eyes of non-believers
                                    follow

how even a sparrow's feather can stand in for grace
while another species bears the name
and fate of pinkened love

how the new-hatched in the nest
                    shards of turquoise shell still stuck
                    to its back
can crack a human heart

O bird   O human heart

NOTES

"These Are the Trials of Water" appeared in *The Malahat Review*; "Ode to Hazel White" appeared in *CV2* and in the anthology *Walk Myself Home*; "After Sudden Rain" appeared in *Eighteen Bridges*; "Interiors: A Brief History of Landscape" appeared in *What Place, and Home*. "Preparing the Way, She Cut the Perches from the Hummingbird Feeder," "Man from Another Country (Hand to Hand)" and "As Close to the Edge (Navigating the Liminal)" all appeared in various Patrick Lane retreat chapbooks published by Leaf Press. Many thanks to these journals and anthologies.

ACKNOWLEDGEMENTS

Much appreciation to Vici Johnstone and Andrea Routley at Caitlin Press for this beautiful publication. Thanks too to Elizabeth Phillips, for her keen and astute editing. Immense gratitude to my partner, Chris Fox, for first and last readings and for her perpetual support for my poetry in this volume and in others. Many thanks to my sister, Donna Sharkey, for wishing this collection into being in the first place and for reading it in the middle phases. And finally, thanks to so many members of the Victoria writing community. I am surrounded by wonderful poets in two writing groups: Patricia Young, Julie Paul, Cynthia Woodman Kerkham, Barbara Henderson, Claudia Haagan, Isa Milman, Beth Kope, Terry Ann Carter and Sue Gee. Thanks to them all for their kindnesses, support and poetic feedback over the past decade.

PHOTO GREG EHLERS

Arleen Paré's first book, *Paper Trail*, won the Victoria Butler Book Prize and was shortlisted for BC Books Dorothy Livesay Prize in Poetry. She has two other books, *Leaving Now* (Caitlin Press, 2012), a novel, and most recently, *Lake of Two Mountains* (Brick Books, 2014), a collection of linked poetry that was awarded the 2014 Governor General's Award for poetry. Her writing has appeared in numerous literary journals and anthologies in Canada. She holds an MFA in poetry from the University of Victoria.

This book is set in Arno Pro, designed by Robert Slimbach.
The text was typeset by Vici Johnstone.
Caitlin Press, Fall 2015.